A Weathering of Years

A Weathering of Years

Carl Hare

IGUANA

Copyright © 2015 Carl Hare
Published by Iguana Books
720 Bathurst Street, Suite 303
Toronto, Ontario, Canada
M5V 2R4

All rights reserved. No part of this publication may be reproduced, stored in a retrieval system or transmitted, in any form or by any means, electronic, mechanical, recording or otherwise (except brief passages for purposes of review) without the prior permission of the author or a licence from The Canadian Copyright Licensing Agency (Access Copyright). For an Access Copyright licence, visit www.accesscopyright.ca or call toll free to 1-800-893-5777.

Publisher: Greg Ioannou
Editor: Carolyn Zapf
Front cover image and design: Carl Hare

Library and Archives Canada Cataloguing in Publication
Hare, Carl, 1932-, author
    A weathering of years / Carl Hare.
Poems.
Issued in print and electronic formats.
ISBN 978-1-77180-129-4 (pbk.) 978-1-77180-122-5 (epub)
978-1-77180-123-2 (kindle) 978-1-77180-124-9 (pdf)
978-1-77180-121-8 (bound)

    I. Title.

PS8615.A7243W43 2015   C811'.6   C2015-902579-6
                                                        C2015-902580-X

This is an original paperback edition of *A Weathering of Years*.

*To all those living still, or in my memory,
who have inspired these poems.*

Contents

Preface ix

SPRING 1

  Nascence 2
    In the tiny sleeping form 2
    Lullaby, our grandson 3
    Lucy's song 4
    Venstøp, Ibsen's childhood home 6
    Young Ibsen's mad aunt, Faster Ploug, tells him of trolls 7

  A Childish Nature (A city boy's pastorals) 11
    The countryside should not be seen without a filter 11
    He had been put to bed as usual 12
    Drowsily the small boy sat in the back 13
    The landscape of the mind forms early on 14
    It was an old untidy garden 15
    Always in the summer 17
    For the boy, spring meant water and mud 18
    The boy's first visit to a farm 20
    Winter was wool and mitts and frozen toes 21
    On a spring night 22
    The boy was breathless 23
    The lake lay still 27

SUMMER 29

  Nursery Rhymes for Adults 30
    Though strangers at first 30
    Sometimes the mind so fair 31

  Music's muse is woman fair (Falk's song) 32

  Would you like to hear my poem? 33

  At a Picasso exhibition 35

- Birthdays 36
  - At forty, joys of family still exist 36
  - Now as your years soon reach your summer's end 37
  - October lights up for your birthday 38
  - On the steep slope below 40
  - Still October leaves present their colours 42

AUTUMN 43

- As in the green dappled forest 44
- How poets scream 45
- Angels spoke to Blake 46
- Sleep slippered, drifting on some dream's dark current 47
- Those ancient Greeks understood it best 49
- For all her lives 51
- His fingers have their own life 53

WINTER 55

- The Ibsen Poems 56
  - Henrik Ibsen and his wife Suzannah 56
  - What Ibsen saw downtown 57
  - Ibsen's song 59
  - Suzannah's creed 60
  - Ibsen's advice to Selma, a young pianist 61
  - Suzannah's advice to Selma and Rebecca 62
  - Ibsen's response 63
- Valentines 64
  - A paradox, this day of love's exchange 64
  - It is said that lovers fall in love, yes? 65
  - As the sea that, tireless, buoys the ship 66
- Seventy 67
  - Who knows what prompts the need for verse? 67
  - But once I stood at that unending water 69

When I see the child of my child asleep 71
How we love the lure of the new scenario 73
Two occasions slip into this fractured memory 74
Indelible some memories remain 76
How memory embellishes the half-life 80
Only two days left before the magic seven 81

Across the bays of the mountain-shrouded lake..................... 82

A New Year's brash imprint 84

Backyard elegy 86

Such union with the inevitable earth 92

Memorials... 94
   Sestina for a ninetieth birthday 94
   On a hundredth birthday.. 96
   The flesh and blood are sloughed away 98
   Music was his breath 102
   The whispered quiver of the leaf....................................... 104
   She is dead now, in her nineties 106

In the dead winter, in the night.. 109

Notes.. 110

Preface

"Who knows what prompts the need for verse?" Most of these poems were inspired by the celebration of specific events, whether births or deaths, marriages or anniversaries, the significance of a year, or the memories of childhood that still slip, uninvited, into the consciousness. The verse forms explore the manner of speaking such experiences, for to me the sounds of a poem, in intimate companionship with its structure, are part of its strength and beauty. I find all species of poems fascinating, but I have discovered that I can write only those that my tongue lets me speak or sing with conviction and sometimes with grace.

The poems fall naturally into the celebration of birth, the urges of youth, the vigour of maturity, and the reflection of age. And as the seasons rise and ebb, then begin the cycle again, so does the book end in the "dead winter" with new life.

The following poems have appeared in publications not normally associated with poetry: "The boy was breathless" under the title "A Young Nephew Visits Carl Lester at a Survey Camp" in the *ALS News* of the Alberta Land Surveyors; "On a Hundredth Birthday" in the *Provost News*; "As the sea that, tireless, buoys the ship" in the *Edmonton Journal*. "Music was his breath" appears on the Malcolm Forsyth page of his music publisher's website at cpmusiclibrary.ca.

My play *The Eagle and the Tiger* is in the archives of the National Library of Norway in Oslo. Excerpts appear in "Spring," Summer," and "Winter."

I have been fortunate in those who have contributed to the growth of these poems, particularly Douglas Campbell, the first to have read and commented on some of them; Sharon Thesen, who not only showed her sensitivity and professional poetic acumen, but also encouraged me to continue to write; Carolyn Zapf, whose close reading and perceptive comments have led to the collection as it stands; and finally my late wife Clara, who spent many hours helping me in the struggle to shape and polish each poem.

SPRING

Nascence

In the tiny sleeping form

In the tiny sleeping form
Lies the future hidden tight,
In the clenched fist still and warm
Hides the vision yet to light.

What behind the eyelid flickers
Current beneath sleeping face,
What betrays the constant fissures
Of the promise and the race?

Helpless now, exposed at last,
Stirred to startle into life,
Peaceful after all that's passed,
Forgetful of the former strife,

In the child is found the woman,
In the birth more births foreclosed,
And the future will illumine
What in the infant is proposed.

But for now she is the focus
Of much love and nurturing care,
In the family is the locus
For parents' and for brothers' stare.

So begins her hopeful journey,
So begins her storied plot
With the brothers in the tourney
Both in action and in thought.

Lullaby, our grandson

Lullaby, our grandson,
Sleep you in peace,
Lullaby, our grandson,
All trouble cease.

In your present world
Of giant shapes
And movement swirled
Of strange landscapes
In which moments
Like drops in fire,
Astonishments,
Quickly expire,

In your soft sheets,
Sense dimly self,
In your heartbeats
Renew yourself,
Let sound and touch,
Taste, smell and sight,
Cultivate much,
Small acolyte.

Your tiny world
Keep with you long,
Your body curled
Relax with song.
Let the giants
Comfort you still,
Your compliance
Gives you your fill.

Lullaby, our grandson,
Sleep you in peace,
Lullaby, our grandson,
All trouble cease.

"Grandson" brings us nearer
To the son again.
"Grandson" makes it clearer
What it is we gain.
In our world the shadows
Creep not in crib but mind
In our world the giants
Cannot be confined.

But your peaceful body
In its crib sustained
For us can embody
Innocence explained,
The leap-frog generation
Keeps the hope renewed
And the animation
In our life renewed.

In your journey's starting
Our destination's seen;
At our silent parting
May your laugh intervene.
All our love rides with you
In your journey long,
All our love we give you
Through this quiet song.

Lullaby, our grandson,
Sleep you in peace,
Lullaby, our grandson,
All trouble cease.

Lucy's song

In my life there is a flower
And that flower is me,
In my life there is a power
And that power is me.

My bud has my own colour
And that colour is me;
No other bud has this colour
And that's as it should be.

Soon my budding will unfold,
Soon the blossom will be seen;
The sight will be as precious gold,
A jewel against the green.

And my scent is like no other
And I will stand straight and tall,
No need to huddle under cover,
I can be seen by all.

Other flowers may stand with me,
Each with its own hue and shape,
But beside them I stand free,
I have my hue, I have my shape.

In my life there is a flower
And that flower is me,
In my life there is a power
And that power is me.

I can endure the wind and rain
I will fight to be me;
I will withstand all the pain
For it is myself I see.

Against the brilliance of the sun
I will not wilt or droop,
And whispers that around me run,
Will not make me cringe or stoop.

In my life there is a flower
And that flower is me,
In my life there is a power
And that power is me.

In my seed I was me,
In my growing I am me,
In my living I am me,
In my discovery I am me.

In my knowledge lies the power
From the kernel to the root,
I know myself for each hour
Nothing else for me will suit.

In my life there is a flower
And that flower is me,
In my life there is a power
And that power is me.

Others may try to divert
Me from myself, make me a lie,
Others may find a way to hurt,
Find the means to make me cry,

But when I doubt who I might be,
If I find I'm forced to cower,
Then I will sing this fresh and free
And in myself I'll find my power.

In my life there is a flower
And that flower is me,
In my life there is a power
And that power is me.

Venstøp, Ibsen's childhood home

The farm ...
A glory and a wonder for me then.
From my attic window not much to see
Except the cool grateful patterns of leaves
Rustling from the great tree close at hand.
But outside, at edge of land, tip of spine,
Oh, the sight of the great lush valley spread
Out before us, gently confined by peak
And sloping sides, summer-rich and hazy.
And on the other side, the path and road long
To any schooling, quietly noisy with beeing
Swarms and bright distractions on either side
Of spine and hill, ripe meadow and field.

For boy, much to distract with puppet and
Game, but dim awareness, sharper questions to
Understand the change from fun to farm, mother
Quiet, father surly, others with queer faces
When met, embarrassment and shame sweating
From walls and people, family and former friends.
First life lesson: a bankrupt pocket means
A bankrupt spirit, family adrift.

But in the house, at open stone kitchen
Fire, warmth in winter in the small steamy
Place melts cold shame and principle to
Simple, basic pleasure and contentment.

Young Ibsen's mad aunt, Faster Ploug, tells him of trolls

(Faster Ploug reaches behind her, where an old sea chest is located, opens the chest, and takes out an old, large book.)

PLOUG
Remember this, my dear?

YOUNG IBSEN
Yes, tante. We look at it every day.

PLOUG
So that you will not forget the *styggemann*.
Show me the picture.
(Ibsen sits on the steps with her, takes the book, turns to the frontispiece. They share the book on their laps.)
There, you see? That's what the *styggemann* can
Look like if you catch him when you turn around.

YOUNG IBSEN
Does *styggemann* have wings? And that funny clump
Of hair on his head? And that scythe?
And that woman holding the big scroll
And that woman with the staff seated on
The throne—they can see him!

(As they continue to talk, soft rustlings, as of fur and claws, can be heard around them.)

PLOUG
No, look, the women are looking at
Each other, not at him! The *styggemann*
Is clever, he knows when people will not
See him, when they do not suspect he's there.
But outside, in the shadows, just behind you,
He waits to grab you, take you for himself,
The dark and awful man!
(She shivers and holds close to Ibsen.)

YOUNG IBSEN
Is he a troll, Faster Ploug?

PLOUG
                        Yes, Henrik,
Although most trolls are stupider than he.
But trolls are dangerous too, dirty, hairy
Creatures, sometimes with one head, sometimes
With more, with three fingers on the hand
And among some, one eye to share.
Some taller than the trees, using sides of
Mountains to sit on, others just as we are
Or smaller, but all mean, stupid, nasty,
Beasts, worse than other animals because
We can see ourselves, our own dark shadows,
In their shambling, sniggering, selfish,
Clutching, boring personalities. The
Hulder men are ugly, ugly as sin.

YOUNG IBSEN
And the hulder women, tante? Are they ugly?

(As Faster Ploug speaks, an unearthly female voice is barely heard singing in the background.)

PLOUG
Oh, they are beautiful, more beautiful
Than the most beautiful of us,
Beautiful as sin. And when they sing on
Midsummer's Eve and Christmas Eve no man
Can resist them. And what they want most is
A human man, a man to marry them,
And when such a man does love and take them
Then their cows' tails fall off and they are
Like us, human like us. And, like us,
They grow old and ugly, only faster,
But if their man is good and faithful,
They are kind and tolerant—if not,

Then they can show their strength and temper
Much more than we. Henrik, be careful,
Look at women closely, watch for the tail,
And beware of their hunger, their passion,
For they can possess you, feed off of you,
Consume you body and soul if they entice
You.

YOUNG IBSEN
(frightened but fascinated)
Are you a hulder, Faster Ploug?

PLOUG
(smiles)
Do I have a tail?

YOUNG IBSEN
              I've never seen you with one.

PLOUG
Hulders hide their tails, tie them up under
Their skirts. But here, feel here, can you find one
Here?
(She directs his hand behind her. He feels timidly.)

YOUNG IBSEN
    No, tante.

PLOUG
            Then I am not a hulder.
(She holds him closer and whispers to him.)
But I know what a hulder feels, what a hulder
Wants, I am driven like them, suffer
Like them, and fear and rage like them.
But you must not tell anyone—this is our
Secret, only you and I know this. Promise
Never to tell what I have told you here.

(Ibsen looks at her, wide-eyed. She holds him tightly, her face close to his, staring into his eyes.)
Here, before the *styggemann*, promise!

YOUNG IBSEN
I promise.
(The singing ceases.)

PLOUG
(hugging him)
          That's my own Henrik!

A Childish Nature (A city boy's pastorals)

The countryside should not be seen without a filter

The countryside should not be seen without a filter,
At least for city children.
At six years, in a small Nova Scotian town,
So distant from his western city home,
He came out of his new-found uncle's shop,
Still enthralled by huge shiny sheets,
Galvanized and booming when buffeted
By tiny, curious fists, and by the mystery
Of dark, heavy pipe in curious shapes
And curves, and by all the cumbrous tools
Of that metallic-smelling trade,
Sensed in the shadowed dark of dusty panes;
He squinted in the new glaring sun
And headed down the street
And screamed.

Ahead of him, at the end of the block,
The world stopped, abruptly fallen away;
No order of streets and shops and houses;
Instead, in what he thought was the town's middle,
Fields suddenly took the place of sidewalks,
He could see into a distance of waving grain
Without the comfort of any structure
To rise above the sea of grasses, trees and shrubs.

Even now this gash in what the world should be,
This shock of betrayed juxtaposition,
Forced an alien accommodation
Upon a stricken and bewildered boy,
That still festers in his later memory.

He had been put to bed as usual

He had been put to bed as usual, but knew
That he was losing his parents for tonight,
And he disconsolately fell asleep.
Then drowsily he awoke as strong arms
Picked him up, still wrapped in blankets,
And took him to the car. He saw streetlights,
Their beams speeding through the car and out,
Then speckled darkness or rushing headlights
Until the car stopped and he was carried
Out to a field that met the stars and night
In all directions except its centre,
Where blazed the fire of the world, immense;
Its flames reached out to fight the blackened field
And to lick hungrily toward the night,
Showering its own stars up forever.

Shadows flickered against the roaring glare,
Faces half-moons shining with thrilled pleasure,
And the boy found himself, his warm cocoon
Now his banquet table, nibbling as he
Felt on one side the crisp fresh night air
And on the other the smoky heat.

The world was born again for him that night
As he sensed the special festive need,
A moment graced, limitless and defined
Between the writhing, evanescent flames
And the immeasurable, inscrutable dark.

Drowsily the small boy sat in the back

Drowsily the small boy sat in the back,
Just able to see through the vibrating pane,
Smelling the dusty, rough-textured seat,
Hearing the coarse hum of engine mixed
With the grating sound of gravel-crushing tires.
Miles of fields and hills rushed by through the glass,
All made golden by a setting prairie sun;
And now the road dipped even as
The sun did; a dusky twilight grew;
The migrant trees turned black,
Cut out against the graying fields beyond.

Suddenly, as tree and field began to blend,
Behind the trees the boy saw, at eye-level,
A thick gray-blue smudge
Spreading ominously to the darkening sky.
Roads by prairie lakes run low, at the level
Almost of the water; the farther shoreline
Of a larger lake cannot be seen;
But for this boy, who'd never seen a lake,
That close, menacing, infinite, unmarked horizon,
Left him at the end of the world,
Terrified that what he feared would thicken,
Creep past the trees, and engulf him
And the speeding car;
That he would be absorbed in some sinister
Way into that growing stain and lose all
Feeling of self, of sense, of anything.

The landscape of the mind forms early on

The landscape of the mind forms early on;
Its terrain looms in the sharp, uncritical glance
Of the child, it seeps into the unprotected
Realms of later dreams, it never leaves him.

So again the undulating hills appear, the car
Again rolling down through the dust
Of ricocheting gravel on the steep, straight
Road, as the clumps of poplar woods
Scatter haphazardly on either side,
Narrowing in the distance to a line,
Small tufts of dust rising along the length.

And for the small boy the colours, all sand,
Browns, yellows, pale silvery greens,
White from small wooden steeple, or weathered
Red on barn, weathered siding on tired house;
But always the sense of the space, the massive hills,
The narrow valley huddled in between,
And cutting through them the straight, straight dusty road.

Sometimes in the dream the terrain can shift,
A new familiar or created territory,
But always, in the abrupt flash of recognition,
In the long moments that it takes
For the car to descend and start the climb
The hills remain etched on the boy's eyelids
As they droop and close.

Both then and now.

It was an old untidy garden

It was an old untidy garden, one
Of five long lots, separated from the others
By a hedge, and divided by narrow
Grass-covered paths that suggested order
In a helter-skelter chaos of flower and vegetable.
In times of weedy desperation, the gardener came
To rescue for a brief time the blossoms and sprouts
Enthusiastic in their bid for blazing wilderness.

He was old beyond measure, gnarled beyond thinking,
Mature mahogany, perpetually bent from tending
Closely to his charges,
And thus the boy could stand and see him eye to squint.
He spoke in a thick English country accent,
Barely understood by prairie ear,
Rough textured as the soil he worked, that,
Combined with grunts and conversations with himself,
Entranced the fascinated boy.

Once the old man took him to his shack
On the river flat, the two trekking to the valley,
One plodding, an "L" upside down,
The other padding along beside for this adventure.
The shack was small, like its owner,
And dark as he was tanned.
Its furnishings were spare, but still the space seemed full
Of objects dimly seen, profuse like the garden.
A cup of tea made and drunk, an unintelligible conversation,
And back they went to the bent man's true element.

The boy had lived among these plants,
The hollyhocks and tiger lilies, flowers and shrubs
Brightly towering over him,
And he had been strangely disturbed

By their lush colours, their fuzzy delicate textures,
The mystery of their parts;
But when the rough stubs of fingers touched them
They ceased to be apart, exotic and unknown,
And became one with the man, the boy, the sky,
Part of the breath and pulse.
And so they have remained until today,
The man, the boy, the garden under the bright blue sky.

Always in the summer

Always in the summer they would make
One visit to the gardens at Oliver.
The car would quietly and slowly move
About the immaculate grounds and beds,
As parents and child looked with admiration
At the ordered extravagance of colour
Grown with such care and thought, displayed
So beautifully against the background
Of the dignified, classic brick buildings.
They did not leave the car to walk within
This paradise but kept windows open
To revel in the rich or delicate scents;
Walking was not considered appropriate,
Because it would bring into mind
What lay behind those tidy walls,
Where the riots of colour swirled within
Twisted and disordered minds, writhing
In the torment of a different world
Which permits no physical escape.
But the child only saw the ordered colours
And smelt the fragrance, and felt dimly
His parents' quiet avoidance of that inner turmoil.

For the boy, spring meant water and mud

For the boy, spring meant water and mud and
The first cracking through the ice of puddles,
Some small and easily negotiated,
Others covering half a field, ready
To break through and overflow the rubber
Boots; and then tramp home in soggy triumph
To show his courage and resourcefulness.

Near the boy's home, his street
Dipped sharply, a sudden small hill;
By the curb of its gravelled road
The spring's melting snow gushed
In steady, tiny torrents,
Shaping the new-made streams
For the boy's delight.

Down the rapids went his grand armadas,
Swirling and bobbing as they navigated
The tortuous route, the boy crouching low
To seize every detail of the journey,
Every jagged rock, the twisting mud,
The sound of rivulets and the muddy
Mix of smells of oil, gasoline and horse,
As his match flotillas—or, on rare occasions,
His sailboat walnut shells with wooden masts
Precariously held firm with candle wax,
The paper sail damply but proudly full—
Braved unimaginable swift dangers
Until they shipwrecked upon the rocks
Or were saved, caught up by giant hand
To start a fresh voyage, a new adventure,
Or in a sudden, fierce and delightful
Catastrophe, fell off the edge of the world
And disappeared between the ominous iron grates
That marked the journey's end.

And when he raised his head, he caught the scents
Of the new-born wind, the dirt and old grass,
The first hint of lilac and caragana,
Dandelion, and saw old toys now rescued
From the snow where they had lain undiscovered
Over the long cold months.

So too the spring of the boy's sprouting senses,
Plant and water, toy and child emerging in the new day,
The renewed year,
Which now germinates only in the memory
Of those first, fresh days, still living and reliving
In the autumn of the mind.

The boy's first visit to a farm

The boy's first visit to a farm
Was a time of bewildered wonder.
Even at the barbed-wire gate, dragged open,
The reek hit him, sharp, damp and pungent,
Sniffed before only in toilets or on the sidewalk
In small quantities and quickly avoided.
But now the stench did not go away at all,
Got stronger as the car moved down the dirt track
And entered the farmyard itself.

About him he saw fences, sheds and barns;
As he left the car, underfoot a dusty yard;
But as he looked, the yard seemed to move,
As did the trees close by, with yellow and black
Creeping carpets, which, when he looked more closely,
Were bristled caterpillars, great masses of them,
Squished under foot and dropping on his head.
And then he could not stop seeing,
Both that creeping flood and each separate
Wriggler, each black and yellow segment
Humped or extended, the strange rounded head
Shifting to and fro, mandibles blindly
Gaping for any edible green thing.

He ran fearfully to the squirming porch,
Wiped his shoes free of the sticky black goo,
And opened the screen door and stepped in,
Treading carefully on worn linoleum.
Again new scents assaulted him, mixed
With the one all-pervading smell,
Wood smoke, sweat, the tang of uncooked foods
And the odour of hard living.

Little more the boy remembers of that visit,
But for years that plague of squirmers
Stained his dream of the farm and land.

Winter was wool and mitts and frozen toes

Winter was wool and mitts and frozen toes
And all varieties of snow,
But for the boy its greatest pleasure,
Only three streets from home,
Was the ravine, steep and winding,
That gashed the city open
And left it high and far beyond.
Those sides embraced the skiers and the sleds,
A place of slithery abandon and of skidding slopes.

Yet on certain days, crisp, cold and bright,
The ravine gave up its quiet treasures to those
Willing to tramp to find its deepest nooks.
There the poplars hung in heavy spikes
Of glistening snow, as underfoot
The thick crust cracked and glittered.
The boy half walked, half waded
Through the dense, coated thickets.
Meandering along the depths, a creek
Covered with its icy sheet could still be heard
In the stillness, muffled but alive,
And farther down broke out, steaming,
The reek of the sewage that it bore,
Assaulting the frigid, neutral air.
Except for such dark broken blisters, the world
Was white, all bushes, logs and trees
Engulfed in snow, frost and ice.

This was the kingdom of silence, broken only
By the frozen snap of twig and crunch of boot.
No horizons here, just towering white sides
Glimpsed beyond the heavy-laden trees and bushes.
This world the boy loved for its timeless intricacy,
Its unexpected frigid sites and pleasures,
An intimate maze of branch and track,
Winding forever at the bottom of its own universe.

On a spring night

On a spring night, the dark air thawing still,
The boy's father took him outside the city
To a cliff's top, where a field's yellowed grasses
Turned black against the sky,
And there they watched as the sky rained stars.
Vast showers of incandescent streaks
Burnt themselves out in the fretworked dark,
Fireworks playing frenetic hide and seek
Across the vast bowl of the night's cosmos.
Father and son stared together, rapt, silent,
Their intimate proximity the guard
Against the annihilating immensity,
So beautiful, so selfless, and so awful.

The boy was breathless

The boy was breathless
With the wonder of it,
Taken by his uncle
To a new world,
A world up north.

For a week he lived
Another life,
His home a tent,
His bed a cot
Beside his uncle.

In the brilliant day
The boy discovered
The tent glowed inside,
Its canvas translucent;
And the boy could see
The wooden drafting table
Covered with plans,
Hieroglyphics of imposed order.
All was neat:
The plans rolled or tacked out,
The strange pencils in their place,
The pens and inks
Quietly in rank,
The means of correction at hand.

At night the light turned inside out,
The gas lamp hissing
As the uncle carefully
Recorded the surveys of the day,
Every move precise, exact,
His the responsibility
For the right-of-way,
The future highway.

The crew ate meals
In the cookhouse,
Towed beside the tents.
The Norwegian cook,
Big and jovial,
Created splendours
Of strange, aromatic foods:
Breakfast dishes
Of transfigured eggs,
Exotic buns and rolls and breads;
For lunch, eaten in the bush,
Huge packets of sandwiches
And alien pickles
And cakes and cookies
And other indescribable sweets.
Dinner was vast,
Thick steaks or roasts or fowl,
Mountains of boiled potatoes
And other vegetable delights,
Topped off with pies and cakes
And, again, less known sweet things.

The cook let the boy
Watch him prepare,
His movements as spare
And precise
As the surveyor's pen,
His strong arms and hands
Working effortlessly.

Once the boy left the ordered pattern
Of tents and caravan
And trekked with the crew.
He walked behind,
Stumbling through the brush,
Wading across shallow creeks,
Arms upraised
To ward off the whipping branches

Or slap the squadrons
Of all-conquering mosquitoes,
Until the procession stopped,
The transit set up,
The measured line pulled taut,
The rod adjusted carefully
Through the delicate sights,
The spikes driven in,
And the square marker pits dug.

The boy, weary after the day-long ritual,
Wondered at his uncle,
Who, after the journey home
And dinner,
Returned to the tyranny of the table,
Working into the night
To make sure the day's results
Were made secure.

One day the boy
Went with the cook
And picked wild raspberries,
The tiny fruit hidden
Or peeping from behind the leaves.
The boy learned to pick
Delicately and surely
And not to eat too many
So that there would be enough
For the crew's pies and other desserts.

On another day
The boy went with the farmer
In whose field they camped,
And they ploughed.
The boy sat on the tractor
Deafened by its racket
And watched the farmer
Lead the plough

Beside the deep neighbouring furrow
To rip another line
In the dusty black earth.
At the end of the long striped field
The tractor etched a curved track
To start another furrow
In a different row.
When the tractor turned
The boy saw the huge swirls and patterns
Carved into the disturbed earth.
The farmer let the boy steer:
He carefully kept the massive ribbed wheel
In the deep adjacent groove
And was the master of the world.
All through this journey
The air was filled with dust,
And when they finished,
Man and boy were blackened,
Only their eyes and mouths uncovered,
But their nostrils clogged with dirt.

But the boy felt he was a man
Now, and that the farmer
And the uncle were akin,
Each wrestling with the earth,
Each making intricate order
Out of wilderness,
And the marvel of it
Never left him.

The lake lay still

The lake lay still
In its dawn-risen splendour,
The water still as ice,
Clear and mountain-blue.
The great mountain
Reared its pyramid;
The trees and water
Nestled close;
The rusty granite sheen
Reflected in the quiet surface.
Around the lake
Tendrils of mist, sleeping still,
Kept mysterious the shores.

Into the lake glided the canoe,
Father kneeling in the back,
Son in the front.
In respect for the sacred quiet
They moose-paddled silently in J's,
Barely a wake betraying their progress.
In the dead centre of the lake
They let the canoe drift,
Their paddles idle,
And drank in,
With absorbed breath,
The lake, the mountain and the shore.

Even the birds remained silent
In this time-stopped moment,
With the sun bringing alive
The sheer rock face,
The water clear and glacially blue,
The air suspended in crisp clarity.

The canoe now eased its way
To the far shore;
They crept along
Until an outcrop thrust its way
Into the still enshrouded lake.

As they drifted by it,
Out of the mists a grey shape grew.
A wolf stood at the outcrop's tip,
And, yellow-eyed, gazed at them,
Motionless.
His coat was dusted in white,
And one hind leg was still clamped
In the teeth of a broken trap.
The three—wolf, father, son—
Remained suspended there,
Eyes locked, without sound, still,
Until, with no apparent motion,
The wolf faded back into the mist
And disappeared.
The canoe drifted on,
But no words were spoken,
Nor were any heard
Until the journey's end.

Later, a warden told them
Of the wolf:
Old and clever, he had
Escaped, trap on his leg,
And had not been seen
The last three months.
But even then little was said.

The lake, the mountain, and the wolf,
And their bond,
Still haunt the memory.

SUMMER

Nursery Rhymes for Adults

Though strangers at first

Though strangers at first
Who meet just by chance,
Two snails' courtship is long,
An unhurried dance.

A delicate meeting
Both wary and shy,
Then touches and stroking
Of taste stalks and eye;

And as their time lingers
They stretch and slip high
Fused as one arch of grace,
Their houses awry.

So two snails make love
In a leisurely way
From the first time they meet,
Then all through the day.

Sometimes the mind so fair

Sometimes the mind so fair
Finds that it cannot wear
Its tattered nerves that shrill
Their shards of pain that never still
And rips them off to kill
The fire   then dissipates into thin air

Sometimes

Sometimes the mind so strong
As it sings its brilliant song
Soaring from its nested place
As nerves and blood within it race
Without warning slams apace
Into oblivion without thought of wrong

Sometimes
No time

Sometimes the mind in its array
Grows tired   no longer wants to stay
Quietly doffs its sensation
Makes its final abjuration
Whispers its abdication
Turns on its side and drifts away

Drifts away

No time
No

Music's muse is woman fair (Falk's song)

Music's muse is woman fair,
Grace of flesh and grace of air,
Mingled fragrance, sight and sound,
Female essence light, profound,
Promises insinuating,
Deep desires resonating,
Hair and note, sweet curve and tone,
Sing their harmonies and hone
Deep within the hidden zone
Contrapuntal pleasures known
Only through the skin and ear
Sounding fugal touches clear.
Never let their mingling cease,
Beauty's sound and beauty's peace.

Would you like to hear my poem?

On that morning the city street was like
Many US city streets downtown,
The office cliffs broken by small meadows
Of parking lots, the traffic moving irritably
With only the occasional swerve
To make the corner accompanied
By harsh loud responses from those aggrieved.
Along a shorter street, three patrol cars
Blocked the passage, the police
Frisking and questioning a black trio, blank faced.
Another street with utter nonchalance
Presented rich and shabby fronts.

As he walked past this panoply
Toward the Mecca of the art museum
A voice called out,
"Would you like to hear my poem?"
He turned to see a girl sitting on a news box,
Her dog sleeping at her feet.
"Would you like to hear my poem?"
She repeated, still perched on her rock.
Intrigued, he moved closer and agreed.

She opened a worn notebook lying on her lap,
Its lined pages laboriously scribbled
With large and childlike letters.
As she read, her sweater sleeve,
Brown and musty, slid to her fingers
With their cracked and dirty nails,
And her young, snub-nosed, freckled face
Stared earnestly at her precious words.
Her verse, punctuated by the roar beside her,
Dealt with the themes of war,
The global threat, the nation

Engulfed in commerce and hypocrisy,
And, more personal, recent betrayal
And the yearning for more intimate connection.

The poem finished, her notebook carefully closed,
He asked about herself.
Unaffectedly she answered that she came
From northern California, had traveled up the coast,
Broke with her boyfriend on their travels,
And now wanted to move inland to Oregon.
The golden Labrador awoke at her feet
And, bored, brushed by him to find a new place
To doze below the news.

He thanked her, giving her a bill as gift,
And wished her well.
As he walked away she called,
Still perched upon her small retreat,
"Have a good day!" and then, hastily amended,
"Have a good life!"
He waved back, walked on,
The contrasts churning in his mind,
And entered the great sleek mausoleum
And lost himself in new antiquities
From a minor place in ancient China.

At a Picasso exhibition

Quietly they stood beside the writhing line,
soft voiced, inseparable,
both dressed in black,
long carefully brushed hair
framing the delicate oval faces,
their slight bodies still
or moving unobtrusively together,
weathering in dark coolness
the fierce onslaught of exploded form,
miasmic colour. With each new vantage
they would appraise the shocked and pungent image,
smiling at their private, secret comments.
How could the tortured bull that raged
in disciplined stroke before them
beat down their calculated sisterhood?

Birthdays

At forty, joys of family still exist

At forty, joys of family still exist,
While you reckon time by decades, not by years:
But yet your art remains the catalyst.

To build your loving home you still insist,
And playful time with wife and child endears:
At forty, joys of family still exist.

And yet the lures of acting do persist
Even with the vagaries of your careers—
But yet your art remains the catalyst.

The lives of parents, siblings, still entwist
With yours, this past's continuance adheres:
At forty, joys of family still exist.

For two decades the treacherous boards you've kissed
Even when no break or chance appears:
But yet your art remains the catalyst.

Now you for this uncertain stage enlist
To try this talent that yet perseveres;
At forty, joys of family still exist,
But yet your art remains the catalyst.

Now as your years soon reach your summer's end

Now as your years soon reach your summer's end,
Your century's split now just a year away,
A celebration on this special day
Of what these years compile should comprehend
Your hard-won values, your full worth commend.
Always you forged your path, seldom astray,
On your own, hard laboured, with small delay,
Struggling for faith, for knowledge, to transcend
The obstacles confronted, and won through.
As the hawk wings against the shuddering air,
Pierces through the tangled brush, seeing there
A movement slight, then plummets to pursue,
So does your quick eye capture the right clue,
In calculation the solution snare,
Around you, sharp understanding, with care
For those you love; insight in all you view.
So near this season's close your strength has made
A family's foundation firm and sound,
Within an eyrie safe; teaching that's true.
Perceptive and canny, never afraid,
Both stern and loving: you have gained high ground.

October lights up for your birthday

October lights up for your birthday
The maples blaze their scarlet message
Across the east for you
Prairie trees quietly respond
With muted rusts and yellows
Spiked with the bright chatter
Of the rowan and its berries
The west coast splashes
Its whole palette for you
With its vast scale of innumerable greens
Backing the foam of other vegetation's colours

And on this occasion
October may celebrate more softly
With air filled with snowy lace
To hush the fussing day
In a white baby blanket

October is patient and generous
It has celebrated your birth
Thirty-four times
And it is quite willing
To go on celebrating
Many, many times

So too as October's leaves
And snow accumulate
Do your autumnal birthdays
Gather force in celebration
Of the spectrum of your life

And I in the true autumn
Of my life with my own
Accumulated days
Can admire and celebrate
Your ever-varied patterns
And sense the rich fabric
Of your lived experience
With love and quiet curiosity
Especially on your day of birth

On the steep slope below

On the steep slope below
the doe and her two fawns,
now her own diminutive size,
with dainty deliberate steps
forage through the yellowing brush
among the dark evergreens.
On a tiny plateau
the doe rests,
ears flicking, alert,
and lets her offspring
graze on their own.

On this October day,
sun flickering through the needled boughs,
the mountain side is like an oil painting,
all thick browns and greens,
only the occasional flash
of reds and yellows
from the deciduous minority.

Soon the brown grasses that coat the slopes
and the ever green woods
will triumph
as the leaves drift gently
from the graying trees
and creeping vines
or are torn helter-skelter
from the thrashing arms
in the harsh October winds.

Sometime soon even the triumphant colours
will be conquered
as a snow of flakes
waft over trees and slopes
leaving no colour.

But each day,
regardless of the colour
and the capricious weather,
the doe and fawns
will return to forage
and to rest,
leaving their tracks below.

Now a decade
and a bit
since celebration of your birthday
in verse,
here is a new salute
with both our worlds altered:
we here on a mountainside
far from the prairie and the city home,
you on another city side
with a husband and a family,
two children
surprising each day,
career shifting
even as the weather.

Let this anniversary
be like the doe's breathing space,
a moment to reflect
in the tumultuous present
and keep your own prints
firm in the changing pattern
of each future season.

Still October leaves present their colours

Still October leaves present their colours,
Parading them before you as they have
These past fifty years. Or the month quiets
The earth with its silent flakes to respect
Your first half century in its embrace.

Here in your late summer you now explore
The fresh springs of your two sprouting children,
Vibrant in thought and act, close in their love,
Tending the garden of their experience
Even as they discover for themselves
The sanctuaries hidden in the grasses,
Trees and vegetation found in the back
Of the hospitable yard of your home.

As well their sports on field and ice, intense
In act, happy in execution,
Husband involved, committed to their time,
And to the long quiet walks with you
In the lingering gaze of the evening sun
Along the quiet paths fringed with tree
And bush, sheltered from the busy streets.

So too in your maturity you wend
Through the paths, convoluted and arcane,
Of your august vocation, by the vaults
Of the nation's massive bank, more secure
For what the future years may then unfold.

Now my eyes, fixed in the descent of winter,
Can still watch with deep-worn fascination
And affection the quickening animation
Of your evolving complex journey.

AUTUMN

As in the green dappled forest

As in the green dappled forest, trunk-gnarled,
A tree soars tall, its reaching limbs dressed thick
With restless leaves, below which young shoots prick
The earth, tree-seeded, and in time unhood
Their own branched foliage, having withstood
The ripping winds, drenching storms lunatic
With lightning, each young tree a maverick,
Yet in the blind loam their roots search for good
Nourishment and together intertwine,
So our daughter and two sons, all unique,
Rise in the family's uncertain shifting breeze,
Apart, distinct, with their own children shine,
While deep the roots of generations seek,
So interlaced within the sheltering lees.

How poets scream

How poets scream
In their anger and despair
But how beautifully they do it

They slash the page with words
They rip the lines in their rage
They search for words to cut
For images to confound the eye
Sounds to whip the ear

To puzzle
They bundle up their meaning
In obscure phrases
Relying on the resonance of relevance
After the reader's laboured research

Single words glow on the page
Gobbets of words spatter arbitrary areas
Rhythm thunders
Or broken
Lurches fitfully to conclusion

At their best
Their cries pierce to the heart
At their worst
They leave a residue
Of irritation and rejection

Their listening world is small
Populated partly by themselves

But they are among our heralds
The true singers of our perilous path

Angels spoke to Blake

Angels spoke to Blake
As a child he saw them radiant
And heard their voices luminescent
Tinged with sun-flaring throats
And they were his companions all his life

What they sang or hummed or ululated
He absorbed rapturously
Whether the meaning of a stalk of grass
Or the glory of the thunder
To let his mind create its tiny heaven

As he grew older
His hand strove to capture them
His mouth strained to echo their cadences
He wielded the coloured print   the written word
Into an ecstatic synthesis

And past the angels' immaculate raiment
And the terrible beauty of their utterance
He saw the world with new-born eyes
Taking his journey past the innocent child
To the smoky horrors of the cities

And the harsh magnificence of jungle
And the shining natural mysteries
And into the domains of the angels themselves
Shrouded in their unfathomable landscapes
And tried to find line and letter for it all

He and his sight were a tsunami
He swept all before him
Family and wife   artifacts and friends
All caught in the wave of his vision
And he finally subsided peacefully
In the spotless laps of his life-long companions

Sleep slippered, drifting on some dream's dark current

Sleep slippered, drifting on some dream's dark current,
I reach toward the unimagined shore
With lassitude, merely a shade observant.

The old engine of the plot, as before,
Grinds forward with more incidents bizarre
And mundane both, emerging from a core

Puddled from old fragments felt from afar
To refurbish stock settings from past dreams—
The dark bungalow, silent, door ajar,

Its evergreen and poplar lawn still seems
To creep dimly to a river where drear
Sedge thickens, a dock, rotted, palely gleams,

All familiar, known but existing only here,
Never in wakened life, lost the dream's mazes,
Only the memory of the scent of fear

Curling through the sepia, spent rooms' spaces
In which small fitful scenes erupt and dance
Their conflicts among half-known, half-seen faces.

Now this protagonist, caught in the chance
Encounter, only struggles to discover
The way through wayward quarrel to advance

Or in strange quiet moments to recover
From sense of loss, futility or rage
Meanings which, impenetrable, hover,

Elude insight; nothing sensible to gauge
The vivid scenes, absurdly logical,
That at each crucial point escape the cage,

The dream stuttering but formidable,
Oblivion or consciousness the state
Before a further lurch inimical.

So do the little dramas permeate
The hazy verges of the drifting mind
To leave it restless, puzzled, enervate.

Those ancient Greeks understood it best

Those ancient Greeks understood it best:
To know someone in the fullest sense
Must happen when the body's laid to rest
And the whole pattern of the life cements
The jigsaw into place, and so ferments
A vision of the moira's full dimension
To give such existence comprehension.

"Know thyself"—a Greek philosopher's behest—
Turns tables, makes the problem more intense,
Forces the mind's eye inward to invest
In ways to know, some harder, some less dense—
To grasp, let's say, at the self's invention
In reputation, name, accomplishments,
Celebrity—mere terms for pretension.

In the same vein, what one does becomes the text
Whether to obey some duty's portents
Or in ethical doctrines to attest
That a good life, good works, is evidence
Of who we are, and fully represents
Us—but this view is still in contention—
Too narrow for full representation.

Modern times have brought the Freudian inquest:
Dissect our thoughts, pore over their contents
To make the seething current manifest,
And show us, surface pierced, as implements
Of subterranean drives, mere extension
Without real identity, live fragments
For whom the self must be misapprehension.

And science also ponders to dissect
Us further, reducing to mere segments
Of chemicals, neurons, all to suggest
We're purely patterns of electrical events.
And yet, despite all, we show resilience,
Define our mask, fight for reinvention,
And struggle for our intimate retention.

For all her lives

Her eyes
sky clear
unswervingly direct
in the observant face
engaged wholly in what is read
and said

Response
to the other mouth
like the flash of a sleek fish
leaping from the long stillness of a pond

Actions
without comment
done for themselves
as an animal pads its way
through the thick mulch of the forest

Much for the other
little for herself
the quiet accomplishment
no recognition needed

So her life beyond the stage

But in the multicoloured light
on the familiar floor
before the dusky cavern
subtle in its shuffling sounds
like those on the beach of a quiet sea
what absorbed before now blazes fierce
lighting the new-born scene
with force of mask and personality

and uttered meaning
to provoke laughter
to instill tears
to shine on one creature
among the crowd that she has shown
over the punctuated years

Let the applause roar
for all her lives

His fingers have their own life

His fingers have their own life, never stop their agitation, always grasp
    a pencil, pen, anything that can impregnate the sheet, the
    envelope, the margins of some document with which he
      spends more time inscribing than reading, or
        his ever-present workbook, stuffed with all
          the creatures of his fertile mind, or
           the products of his sharp
              eye, accurate,
                witty,
              devastating
           in their visual truth.
            How many
             drawn
              or
         can   we   really
      even
          imagine the thousands
          upon thousands
                    over
           the years? And
           his quick luxuriant
           painting, his rich
           imagination seen
         in his extravagant and
       unique costumes, his sets,
     glorious, resplendent. A great designer, one
   whose designs shall still continue unabated, and
whose bright startling vision may not be seen again.

WINTER

The Ibsen Poems

Henrik Ibsen and his wife Suzannah

Small rented spaces were their lairs
to which she soared
clutching her prey
to bring him prowling to deliver
to digest
to provide the larger boundary
for his inner world
so bright
so clear
within his mind
to let the words bite on the page
as she
perched firmly
in the shifting temporary space
guarded him
cared for his needs
endured his roars
and wracked her body
wrecked her voice
in the never-ending vigil
The rewards did not reach her perch

What Ibsen saw downtown

SUZANNAH
So, my Bear, and what did you see downtown?

IBSEN
Well, my Cat, I met a man.
After the café I saw him seated
On a bench as I walked back, and so
I sat down with him, at the other end.

SUZANNAH
What was he like? Who was he?

IBSEN
                                          A shabby
Man, with thick black jacket, dirty pants,
A seaman's rough wool cap, craggy lined face,
Unshaven, seaman's eyes, liquor scented,
Out of work, out of luck, buying only sunshine
On the bench, spending time under the trees.

SUZANNAH
Why did you sit beside him? You with your
Good clothes on! Uff da! Ibsen!

IBSEN
There was something—raw and fine about him,
A sea-spawned solidity and dignity,
Wildness and patience combined with steady
Gaze, a face in which the skull burned through the skin.
We sat there, silent, on bench ends, absorbed
In sun and air, breeze and bird, flower and leaf.
He broke silence first.
"You go this way each day," he said as fact,
Not question. "You walk like a sea-captain
I know, but in different clothes and different
Circumstances." Silence again.

I glanced at him. Old, an ageless old,
Fifty or a hundred. "Still a seaman?"
I asked. He smiled and did not smile—creases
Rock solid, unmoving. "No more," he said,
"Legs gone, sea gone for me, only drink left,
And sun, when there is any. And memories."
"How long at sea?" I asked. "My life," he said,
No regret, just fact. "Where have you been?"
"All seas and oceans, all continents, all
Islands, ports, bays, tributaries, beaches.
Storms and calms, cold and hot, gales and breezes.
All sail, avoided steam, closer to the sea
That way, sniffing out the way, tacks and straight ahead.
Days of boredom, ports of riot, drinking off
The pints of blood to link with seamen past,
North, and present—in the blood to drink the blood.
And you?" he asked. "My relatives' profession,"
I said, "not mine." Conversation ceased.
The sun took over for a time. We sat
At our respective bench ends, in solitary
Companionship, linked by sun and mutual
Kinship, rough hands and fine gloves antiphonal.
And in that moment I sensed the great harsh
Wooing of the sea, the need for freedom,
The unknown, the breaking from the cosy bond,
Life in the shadow of wet, anonymous death,
To be alive with danger, to endure,
To seek and not to care for finding.
But then time started up once more, my watch
Was out, off bench, a nod, and then back home.

Ibsen's song

In our spring the urge for woman
Is a torrent of desire
Lashing us to find and conquer
Heeding only need for fusion.

In our summer urge remains still
But a river more directed
Relationship is now expected
Soul with soul can take its fill.

In our autumn urge continues
Current in a pebbly stream
Foams against stressed self-esteem
Aches along with tired sinews.

In our winter urge is hidden
Like a tide beneath the waves
To emerge from psychic caves
Unexpected and unbidden.

Suzannah's creed

My family, my life, all or nothing.
Not what I imagined or intended, but
What I said that I should do if married.
And I have learned, learned to my very nub,
That each day the loving battle must be
Joined, each day the fresh idea, sharp image
Must be found, planted and harvested
In growing seed for his own slow reaping.
Childhood delight in book has now become
Daily ablution of the mind, still loved
But put to use, reading to cause writing,
Thought to provoke action, talk at a meal
The insemination of the dramatist.

Two lives always for me, the struggle
Always to let wife work, mind increase,
Two worlds inhabited, constant immigration
Between; and, in the centre, Ibsen.

Ibsen's advice to Selma, a young pianist

If in your music you can find yourself, then
Let your struggle centre there, but be sure
That is where you find your truth and value.
The struggle for the form and meaning
Will never end, but in that obsession
May lie your own living sense of purpose
And in that forging fire, fulfillment.

Suzannah's advice to Selma and Rebecca

Fulfillment ... yes. To find yourself through
Your own voice and act: to know the vision
And the purpose and to follow them.
For you the gift is there to use or lose.
Rebecca,
For you the power lies in the ego
And the body. I have not had your face;
Selma, I have not had your hands.
I have no voice; I live with Ibsen,
An instrument in his orchestra.
But neither of you yet
Knows the price of compromise, of what is
Given up to find the goal, as I do.

You both must make your choice to act and not look
Back, but careen down with the avalanche.
Just make sure that purpose you have chosen
Is worth the price that you will surely pay.

Ibsen's response

The avalanche takes both men and women.
Women feel and fear men's power—but men
Themselves, when half asleep, through slitted lids,
See baby-eyed past glittering sheen power's
Fragility, ephemerality,
Then past that card-built tottering edifice,
Past the almost moving, blue sinister
Curtain to where the closet shadows lurk,
Waiting, the unnamable fears that twitch men
To conceal them in the flannel trappings
Of power's many guises: the brute force
Of frightened, violent, tender ego,
Or the more complex, no less destructive
Force of money, politics, aggrandizement
In all its forms.

Valentines

A paradox, this day of love's exchange

A paradox, this day of love's exchange,
Its past reeking of martyrdom and death,
Pagan and Christian eros in one breath
Commingling, emotions loosed to tightly range.

And in the well-worn stories, great lovers strain
To overcome their hardships, their passions thwarted,
To keep their troth from many sides distorted,
And glory in the end in their shared gain.

So we, now in rough age's quickening sand,
Must live with absence, staunch memory's prick,
Find solace for the urge too quickly killed,
And in this seventh decade's bann demand
Our right to make our love's diminished wick
Flame with new flare, its purity distilled.

It is said that lovers fall in love, yes?

It is said that lovers fall in love, yes?
As if we plunged headlong over some cliff
Or tripped to drop onto the ground, too stiff
To stop the descent, but land in distress

And confusion, as if the shock of love
Is too sudden, blossoms torn by the wind.
And after the fall, what then? Our state limned
By this one feeling, taking no note of

The duration of time after the fall,
The years that pass in love not in free flight,
Decades elastic with emotions full,
Volatile, contradictory above all,
And ourselves, drenched always in this brash light,
Stilled by love's tough, insidious pull?

As the sea that, tireless, buoys the ship

As the sea that, tireless, buoys the ship
Making its long way, forging its spread wake
To find the harbour it must undertake;
As the earth nourishes the silent pip
And lets it through the fecund surface slip
And its blossom, with colour ripe, awake;
As the sky vision's cloudy drift can shake
Into such fantasies that will outstrip
The heavy grounded thought to soar swift, free;
So through seasons evanescent do you
Shape our bauble world, sustain its twisting flight,
Nurture each seeded thought toward its act,
And commove fancy to wrench time askew
In this old universe to gift our love anew.

Seventy

Who knows what prompts the need for verse?

Who knows what prompts the need for verse?
The flicker of an eyelash,
The shock of recognition,
Abrupt invasion of an ancient memory,
A sound or colour to pierce the heart,
Insidious shifting of words emerging from a dream:
All provocations for this strange impulse.

So the meaning appliquéd to numbers
To give the prescribed stages of our life significance:
As in the hour of birth,
The recognition of budding adulthood at sixteen,
The citizen's twenty-one,
The stigmata of thirty, forty, fifty,
And the shock of sixty-five's release.

And seventy?
As a road winds in unexpected turns
Up from the sharp inclines of a valley,
Resonant with its streams,
Up through the darkening trees,
Up to the rock and snowline,
To twist again and perch for a moment
At the divide, the watershed,
Before a tortuous descent,
New cataract and streams
Careering to their final destination
In the vast, anonymous ocean,
So too this particular year
Is the signature for my devious route.

Janus-headed I see the past and future
Terrain of this still evolving landscape:
Down the familiar slope I glimpse
The patchwork fragments
Of the multitudinous years;
Down the incline yet to be traversed
I cannot see the crevices or landslides
That may engulf, annihilate,
But only the thin hazy shore
Of that anonymous sea.

But once I stood at that unending water

But once I stood at that unending water,
Lingered briefly on its sullen shore,
Steeped foot-deep in its deadly chill.
Fifty years ago the incident took place:
The van raced along the gravelled road,
Myself a temporary passenger,
Until a sudden swerve,
A driver's muffled exclamation,
And then a vicious tilt,
The windshield rushing at and through my face ...
A tank trucker saw it happen:
The van, far too fast, skidded, shifted,
Then began a shattering dance,
Leaped from the road
And rolled over five times
In that northern muskeg.

After it settled, upside down and thoroughly crushed,
I remember rising, one eye sealed shut by blood,
To touch three rusty dents on the girdered chassis,
Or so it seemed to my hazy, myopic eye.
But in that moment what still stays with me
Is an extraordinary stillness
In which each sound is magnified:
The rustle of my clothes as I reach
And the very sound of my touch
On the rusty metal
And even, in that eternity under my feet,
The minute rustle of each blade of grass.
There was, in that radiant instant,
A rebirth of all experience, the world renewed,
And I with it.

The aftermath remains with me as well—
The car flagged down,
The trip to district nurse and then the hospital,

The argument who should wear the two remaining unmatched shoes,
The ear sliding cold and slick along my downturned face,
The hypodermic week in hospital—

But that one key moment
Remains epiphany,
The separation of my early life from all the rest
As that deadly flood receded
To await an inevitable return.

When I see the child of my child asleep

When I see the child of my child asleep
There in her crib, her features in repose,
And see the traces of our selves still keep
A history from declining to a close,
Then I must face again that no one knows
From whose womb I started, and whose blind seed
Sparked repetition of a line of those
Whose hidden lineaments must still feed
The void of my aching ignorance, my deep need.

The stories of our lives must have some start
Even with the birth of an illicit son
Rejected by his mother's fearful heart.
Yet here the incident begins to run
Another way. To make the tale fine-spun:
In that same hospital a woman pale,
A former nurse, had borne a still-born son,
And nurses switched the dead for new-born male
To let their friend, miscarried twice, a live son hail.

At least, that tale has formed from scattered hints
Collected over time—nurse/mother found
A time for youngster gently to convince
He was adopted, with a love profound.
For years he lived heedless, on secure ground,
Until his daughter from "grandfather" heard
The revelation of the switch that crowned
The origin with romance absurd,
An old man's fancy—or conviction of true word?

To base my life on ambiguity
Forces me, perplexed, to take a double view:
No hindrance from the past, leaving me free,
Unshackled from those ancient ghosts who
Could warn of old disgraces struck anew;

Yet, hidden deep, lurking within the cell,
Lie genetic, fateful, forces, which can rue
The present time, create an unknown hell;
Two journeys to consider, neither settling well.

How we love the lure of the new scenario

How we love the lure of the new scenario
To dream another pattern to the route we go.
To choose at each important juncture a new way
More pleasant, profitable, profound—who can say?

In my own life such fateful forks are clearly seen:
The strange adoption could have changed to orphanage;
More disciplined love could have led to sharper edge;
Small unused award consolidated deeper learning,
More focus, more opportunity, less vague yearning;
Different choice of study; casting won a great stage;
Marriage, the new country, new training, and new offers,
Career kept on stage, not what academia proffers—
New lifelines welling up, all prompted by a hope
That somehow this new history would better cope
With all the failures, struggles, rages, pains and strife
That scar and stain the luster of this present life.

But such dreams are mere evasions to conceal
The truth that in them pain would still be just as real.

Two occasions slip into this fractured memory

Two occasions slip into this fractured memory,
Both catching at the way our minds can play:

I, adolescent, late at night, still in bed,
Begin to sense the nonsense of infinity
In time and space.
What is beyond the universe? Beyond that? And that?
How far does time extend—and either way?
And in the dark, the mind speeding
Past imagined unimaginable limits,
Nausea overtakes and saves him
From the black, black hole.

Decades later, I stroll down
A quiet, tree-shrouded, leaf-patterned walkway,
Lined with university residences, old houses,
In the scented air, the only sound my shoes
Scrunching on some wayward dirt.
I feel the tall greened limbs tunneled
Before, above, behind me,
Myself not only framed,
Inserted in this civil wilderness,
But caught in an illimitable confusion,
Part of what lies beyond the trees, the sky, space itself,
Conceived space, a solar system
Wrenched from the comfortable ego's view
To wander in its orbits in a vast galaxy,
Itself a pinprick among other constellations,
All etched by an ancient light
Provoking imagination to find a source,
Desire some beginning, look to some end,
Dream through hieroglyphics,
Curvature of space itself,
Definition of the unimaginable;

Then down below the shifting canopy
To sense the neighbour organisms,
Down, down to the cells,
Farther, past the chromosomes, the molecules,
The atoms, their flashing, circling electrons,
Deeper, to the realm where imagined order
Gives way to imagined chaos of particles,
Entitled strings, paradox lurching to paradox,
No nonsense this time, but a vast schemata,
All elements perceived at once,
Even as the foot treads quietly
Along the green-leafed street.

Indelible some memories remain

Indelible
Some memories remain,
Burnt free of irrelevance,
Lurking to ambush
The unsuspecting mind.

Our rented house lay undecided
On two diverse slopes:
Behind, the land fell away to meadows, woods,
At night, dark, dark.
The second floor with rooms off the landing
Swung round the walls;
Our bedroom dressed
Like many British bedrooms
With bed and night stands along one wall,
Facing the gas radiant
Flanked by burly English wardrobes;
The left wall backed the dresser,
The right a bookcase and
Windows facing the remote estate.

One Friday night
The train deposited us in Gravesend late,
And late to bed,
Out with the lights,
And darkness everywhere.
Then, to one half-shut, drifting eye,
From the blank corner next to
Window, wardrobe, ceiling,
Emerged a shape
Absent of any light,
Tattered, obscenely holed
Like an ancient lace tablecloth
And chilled past comprehension.

In erratic flight,
With bat-like fluttering,
It came to hover
Over the bed,
An indescribable horror,
And the light in that eternal instant
Finally blazed on
And the thing disappeared.
A nightmare?
When questioned carefully
My wife described it without prompting.
From then on
The hall light was left on,
The room warmed by a comforting dimness,
All objects clear and in their place.

Three weeks passed by.
Again, late train, late bedding,
Again the eyelid on the way to sleep,
When through the wall above the radiant
Drifted forward, slowly, effortlessly,
The height of a tall man,
A single, glowing strand
Of double-coned beads,
Each fist-sized,
Each a transcendent blue.
This time no horror, dread,
But wonder at unearthly beauty;
This time the journey was direct,
Slow, gently deliberate
Until, its destination the bed's foot,
It quietly and gradually dissolved.
This time no need for frantic light switch
But again the careful questions,
Again, agreement.

I studied elsewhere
Joining the family on weekends
When London excursions
Led to the late trains.

Three more weeks gone,
And Easter Thursday came;
I had come home
Before the weekend began.
Late night, late bed,
The drooping eyelid;
When beside the bed and bookcase
Appeared unhurriedly
And without apprehension
A man in a brown business suit
And wearing what appeared to be a white turban.
He gave a friendly smile and wraithed away
In his own timeless fashion.
Again the questions
But this time new response.

"He comes every night
When you are gone."
Every night throughout each week
She had seen this figure standing
Quietly at the foot of the bed
But never had felt fear.

Easter arrived.
Unknown to us,
An ocean and a continent away
An elderly man,
Tea in his hand for his wife,
Dropped dead.
And all nocturnal visitations
Ceased.

When the widow came back to Gravesend—
In quiet conference with my wife
She indicated that this bedroom
Had been her husband's room
And that he always wore a white night cap.

Who knows what all this means?
The children of our family
Complained of seeing "eyes in fire"
Comfortably explained by their curtains,
Rose patterned;
But they also described shapes
Outside their second-story window
Seen against the blackness of the night.

It makes, of course, a good tale to relate,
But still the memories return
To haunt.

How memory embellishes the half-life

How memory embellishes the half-life
Between the dream and wakefulness.

On this occasion new jolt
To old accustomed semi-consciousness.
The usual bed backed to the wall,
Above, at head, the slanted gable.
Lying there, face toward ceiling,
Still unopened eyes snapped open
At a silent noise, sibilant, unrecognized.
Through the gabled ceiling, above the face,
Slowly slid a snake, intently eyed,
Its mouth agape, its sinuous trunk
A glowing, livid green.
Quietly it moved closer to its paralyzed prey
Deliberate, unhurried.
Only at a last moment
Did the still cemented eyes open
To snap shut the vision
And give support to the shaking, sweating body.

So the memory re-evokes the scene
Re-animates the quickening pulse and breath;
But what primordial impulse
Brought the first creation
Or what meaning lies behind the too ready symbol
Neither memory nor ingenious calculation solves;
Only the frozen terror keeps its place.

Only two days left before the magic seven

Only two days left before the magic seven
With its attendant zero, is replaced
By a less resplendent year, and erased
The forced impetus and need to leaven

The shifting weight of three score years and ten
Through musings, recollections told and graced
By verse searching out its meaning, and laced
With ancient memories relived again.

But though the reason for the verse is lost
And the decade's slow decline still moves on
And other shocks prod a new aged fight,

Yet in the yeast of these endeavors tossed
The old bardic exercise prompts more song
And dimmed and haunted thoughts must find new light.

Across the bays of the mountain-shrouded lake

Across the bays of the mountain-shrouded lake
The geese soared, black against the water and the sky,
Heads intent, thrust forward on elongated necks,
Their wings steady, propulsive for the streamlined bodies.
The line flew steadily, all birds in their precise slots,
Heading south, all energy directed to the purpose.
Behind them, another line arced gracefully to a bay,
Then circled back to maintain the route.

Only two lines swept by our mountainside;
But months before, most of the continent distant,
With a small child I stood and counted for an hour.
High, high over the land, line after line
Soared through the dark, dusk-riven sky.
Some sped in small groups of three or five,
Others in larger lines vee'd to a leader,
Still others in squadron after squadron.
The small child watched in wonder,
And we played games of who could first spot the next,
And they flew on with intense focus
Into the darkening sky.

And as I watched, small hand in mine,
I thought to a time so many years ago,
My small hand in my mother's
Hearing the great drone
And looking up to see the sky filled with aeroplanes
All in formation, all moving with the same focus
To the north and to the east
As they soared from Edmonton toward the distant war.

And I thought, as the geese continue in their flight
Some will drop to the hunter's gun
As will some planes in attempting their allotted task;
Only the outcome will be different
When they achieve their destination.
And my old hand pressed gently the small warm hand
As we watched the great flight pass over into the dark.

A New Year's brash imprint

In the exploding night a new year's brash imprint;
as with the slough of snakeskin a glistening, a new gloss,
distracting us with its strong thronged feathered lure
to shape a formless year's progression through the word,
piecing out our hopes, our fears on the jig-sawed shield,
our mind's eyeing of a mindless void.

With what pleasure we take pains to void
the thought of thought, using our ware still to imprint
elaborate convolutions, mind-struck, to shield
against unwary absence, each nudged to gloss
experience in shifting lights, and so to word
ourselves asleep, then awake to lure

back the light. Outside I see the lure
of the great lake's sinuous beauty, making void
this lurch to vertigo. It really needs no word
to speak the shifting blues; mountains loom to imprint,
tree furred, peaks dusted white, cradling the lake, their gloss
beneath the heavy sensuous shield

of drifting clouds, dark bottomed, a shield
ephemeral, smokily edged, vaporous lure
to lose myself, enveloped, still, in its lush gloss,
suspended in its wispy currents, milky void:
no sense of breadth, depth, weight disturbs its mottled imprint
to hood me from the vanishing word.

As twists the falcon, so too the word
wheels back, thought against thought, to rip away the shield
of meaning, sign and symbol in its clawed imprint
struck to their marrow, too broken to withstand the lure
that hurls them, scattered fragments, down towards the void
that in their rents discloses its dark gloss.

New year light prompts once more the body's gloss,
reminder of the reign given sensual word
as flesh and blood, bone, sinew, organs, flood the void
with synapse sparking, signals arced to nerves, to shield
through coiled passages of brain from the illusory lure
of chaos fought by senses' massed imprint.

So I let mind imprint this new year's gloss,
paint this vivid lure so constructed by the word,
and once more hoist the shield to greet the void.

Backyard elegy

Two backyards found in this frigid season
in two Ontario cities visited:

Toronto's in a huddled neighbourhood
of narrow duplexes, behind which yards
trail back to meet adjoining fences
with comfortable small lawns summer edged,
with beds of flowers of many colours
and most shaded by large elms that ignore
boundaries to overhang each other.
Decks large and small join house and lawn throughout,
and foliage shelters where a roof leaves off.
Here is the private world, the miniscule plot
where life persists, thoroughly tamed
for comfort and enjoyment. But now leaves
and buds are gone, save for tattered remnants,
snow slips easily by the naked branches
or rests upon those gnarled outreaches.
Brick and grey and white are left, except for
the scamper of black or brown squirrels,
the gingered padding of cats, the shapes
thick and dark, of ubiquitous raccoons.
The snow is for the children of whatever age
for snowmen and snowballs and splattered faces.
But, left alone, it sucks out the life around it,
shows stark the limbs and fences girdering each space
and is shunned or ignored.

In Kanata the crescent is fringed
with large new houses, most barely into
a second decade, with sleek lawns tended
front and back, trees young and quickly gaining
confidence. This backyard is wider if not longer,
on a slight rise, defined by a cast iron fence.

Here past the deck the yard is split
by a low ancient ridge resisting change,
edged by machine and blast, on which are spread
the Norwegian fir, linden and poplar,
sumac and raspberry bush, and below
upon the tiny lawn the white birches,
red maple and honey locust, all youthful.
Here the snowed clouds, blanketing the sun,
cast dull shadows on the bland snow,
distinguished from the heavy dirty clouds
by its whiteness and the soft textures
of its undulating surfaces
smothering plants, grasses and stone dormant
beneath. The wrought-iron fence holds back
the tangled maze of bushes, trees behind,
and the tended plots on either side.
Snow and jangled limbs and rigid twigs
breathe the cold at those observing them,
even when the sun, bright, pitiless, sparks
the diamond glitter of deep frozen snow.

So distant in the memory, that yard,
beside the ancient bungalow, in which
the boy stood, aiming the hose that had been
unwound so carefully, attached once more
with fingers congealing in frigidity
as now the water hiccupped out, then flowed
to cover the old worn grassed tennis court,
scraped bare of snow, that outlined with its banks
the flooding rink. The boy watched for a while
the creeping surface, let his breathing fog
play about his mouth and nose, then glanced at
the dark tall evergreens that brooded over
two picketed sides, and at the trellised fence,
on third side, forlorn in tattered paint,
a wisp of snow edging its fringe. In this
shade of a place the rink grew firmer day
by day in cold and occasional snow

to bear the weight of uncertain and
unsharpened blades, the cold air now a friend,
crisp, fresh in its rush, with the scrape of skate,
slap of stick, the thud of body on
the unforgiving surface in this time
of young exhilaration. Outside these
pickets, just around the corner beside
another yard, the ditch filled deep with snow,
along the bank of which the boy burrowed
for the hideout of a cave, the pliant snow
just that consistency to hold the shape,
the woolen mitts that mined it caked thick,
as he crouched in the dim interior,
thrilled with the effort and the danger.

But in this time now, this Kanata yard
pictured through the warm kitchen's window
or outside while standing, muffled, on the
whitened lawn, eyes obstructed by perimeter
of fur and hood, braced against the insistent
wind, glasses turning the landscape into
mist, all seen swiveling, as a camera pans,
the whole expanse ice cubed. No trudging past
the ridge, the snow deep or treacherous,
the trek without point.

Perhaps in summer, following the kids
as they gamboled through the wild tall grasses,
pushing through their savannah, their bushes
and the lower branches and twigs, to find
farther back the small raspberries treasured there.

Perhaps in such a fecund time is found
the selfless wonder of this little world
as in that old yard, where, the other side
of the trellis fence, were ranged against it
in an untidy row the graves of pets—
turtles, small and green; unlucky rabbits
who had escaped to find graver dangers;

budgies and canaries, accidental
sparrows and wrens, all now snug together,
their little mounds and tiny wooden markers
weeded over by inexorable growth,
all with names forgotten, but with their earth
still fragrant with its living cover held
in the small nostrils. Or on the uphill
side of the bungalow, the much larger lawn,
haphazardly mown by the boy struggling
with a large iron reel lawnmower
that banged against the ancient roots
which writhed up above the grass beside
their trees, shedding in autumn leaves,
copious in quantity, that were raked
into obliging piles in which to plunge
wildly, to be buried, fully encrypted,
the brown leaves with their dusty smell lying
tissue light upon the face and body.

Why must the mind fix filters to the eyes,
cushion the senses of the aging body,
to make dim the wonders of perception?
Naming the trees, the plants, flowers, grasses,
drifts between each and that first startled sight,
first touch and scent upon the vibrant air;
then the vision of the roots, thick and long,
creeping, sluggish, deliberately slow,
under the soil, around the pebbles
nestled there, extending to support
each tree in the web-strung dark, insistent
against any object; and the flowers
and the weeds with their long fine tentacles
stubbornly in place. The view still finer,
slugs and ants, worms, flies and mosquitoes,
in the thick jungle of the grasses.
Down to the substance of each live thing,
past the bark and pith, stem and carapace
to the realm of cells so intricately
merged together.

Now beyond the senses
only images in machines
traces found through the quivering arms
of the dials
and conjecture
The molecules
planetary systems of the atoms
And whirling
or not
within each
more elementals
protons, electrons, neutrons
and others whimsically named
quarks
pi mesons

And past nanoseconds
    to where time shrinks back
  in the hurly-burly of variants
        and disordered orders
where the mind conceives
        in the simple image of a string
inconceivable dimensions
     parallel universes
  quantum possibilities

And as the synapses of our neural pathways
snap and spark with these electric thoughts
the senses bring us back to the yards
past and present
Eyes rise up to see the dirty clouds
and again new neural journeys
explore the enveloping atmosphere
with its reminders of corrupted elements
that infiltrate the sky and corrode
the equilibrium of the present day
provoking the shiver of apprehension
behind which dread is neatly shelved

So the man
encrusted with the sediments of thought
yearns for that unthinking boy
so caressed by the still
or rustling existences
in the midst of which he stands
Now only memories left
Only the faint tug of those early days
against the blank whiteness
of the present snow

Such union with the inevitable earth

Soft pale flakes
fell through the night,
miasma in tattered light,
quilting the firred, pined limbs
and cotton batting the leveled lawn
compiled against the mountain's slope.
Later the night unflaked, cleared,
her moon exposing a virgin coverlet
unsullied, softly blank
within its black link fence,
only the retreating shadow
of its single great central fir
staining the radiant surface.

But in the morning-after light
a path of tracks skirts from gate
along the edge of the smothered house's
rocky beds to end at woodpile.
There the imprints are clear,
each step quietly, confidently placed,
the snow yielding briefly, crisply
to the almost human print.
Only a streaked depression
Betrays the disappearance of a frozen mouse.
The rutted path shows several came,
and in retreat one cut away,
then back to its comrades
in a curving, patterned line.

So clearly paced, the rut and mark
much like the animals that made them,
a wily family of raccoons
secure in the absolute unthought curiosity
of their winding and acquisitive journey,
no step unneeded, each at home
on the compliant surface

like the graceful stepping
of a great actor, feet at home,
the stage obedient, faithful
to the light, firm ownership;
or the twisted whorls,
the gaps of leaps,
the distorted but beautiful
placements of the dancer,
creating convoluted patterns
on the dazzled surface.

Nor do the raccoons change gait
in other circumstances.
Once, discovered in the garage
having taken advantage of a vulnerable opening,
caught in the glare,
the two upholstered bandits
looked at their discoverer with masked eyes
bared their canines
in a rapacious grin,
then deliberately ambled down the sloping path
toward the gathered darkness,
pausing to turn, each comfortably with the other,
to look boldly and inscrutably back,
eyes shining in the accusing light,
before unhurriedly continuing their arrogant
and sardonic retreat.

How much effort, practice
do we need to achieve such precise,
such complete sallies,
such union with the inevitable earth?

Memorials

Sestina for a ninetieth birthday

The best attempt to celebrate this year,
A decades-encrusted birthday, is with wit,
And for these ninety years keep well in mind
A man who made his latter years an art—
A true feat in this surly quicksand age
In which celebrity detracts from worth.

And therefore herein, for what it is worth,
Let us examine in this special year
How he has marched, triumphant, to old age,
Keeping in mind his riches great, to wit
His love for, and commitment to, all art,
And the tough virtues of his questing mind.

In those first decades, how could not he mind
The need to help his students find their worth,
To search and struggle, work at the art
Of writing, understanding, year by year,
Thrusting them forward through his own keen wit,
Saw them find knowledge as he saw them age.

Yet then it was for him a rough, bluff age
To beat out the treasury for the mind,
Negotiate and fight with all his wit
For a fine-tuned department of real worth,
Until there crashed down one dreadful, fateful year
In which he resigned, despite all his art.

Yet since then, he has had more time for art:
To read, to travel, happily to age,
To find new paintings, make every year
A rich sumptuous garden for the mind

In which he could explore new realms of worth
And discourse to friends with eloquent wit.
Nor have these decades dulled his rapier wit
Nor lessened his perception of his art,
And with shrewd study he increased his worth
To let his finances mature and age;
And he increased the boundaries of his mind
As one by one have grown each generous year.

And so this year will still inform his wit
And still his mind can contemplate his art
And his rich age define for us his worth.

On a hundredth birthday

The old bull is not dead yet. Sunk deep within,
His will to live sustains the ancient days
And lets him drowse past rooms awaiting death
To live again the untold thousand days and nights
Century long, past and present fusing
Child and adult, outside our normal ken.
Recollection works with misplaced memory,
Fragments of now lip up in the flare of wit,
Those around him well-known strangers but for brief
Illuminated moments, and the burden
Of a hundred years lifted from the unsuspecting back.

The outward show of years betrays the deep history
Of what was then and led to now:
The early, fjord-riven wonder of the child
In toil and play on mountain meadows,
Hay scented, snow dominated, the joy of Christmas
Laboriously constructed by his pious father's tools;
The aching absence of mother early dead;
The wild youth-ridden dance and sweep
Of hope and boisterous fun;
The labour with the baked clay, brick,
Inculcated with the skill of masonry;
The gamble to cross seas and oceans
To the unknown, his future bride left,
Then the toss and bride both won;
The change to black, rich prairie clay,
The steady, hard-worked route
Of marriage, farm, and children,
The gradual withdrawal from that which he best knows,
The sky, the soil, the wheat, the seasons,
Wife and one child now deceased,
Then lodge to nursing home.

Celebrate the rich harvest of his determined life:
His mastery of the farming mystery,
The teeming numbers of his many progeny;
His own still-admired character,
And his inclusion in the select club
Of those who earned their hundred years.

The flesh and blood are sloughed away

The flesh and blood are sloughed away
To let the bright light of memory through
To shine on the glistening structure
That we now forge for him.

He would be happy to work it himself—
The idea, the sketched plan,
The shards of metal stroked and picked with care,
And then the pleasure of the labour.
Hephaistos, that old crippled forger,
Would have enjoyed him
Among the brazen fires,
Each sweating happily
On their splendid artifacts.
Daedalus too, his ancestral father:
They would have been contented,
Their self-ornamented goblets in their hands,
Talking through the night,
Then with their nimble knowing fingers
Cutting and carving and twisting and shaping
Yet more births into the astonished air.

Our breathing world he mined
For all that it was worth,
Absorbing it with fascinated curiosity
To create his own world;
And he reveled in them both,
Drawing from what he saw
And what he then imagined.
Everything he did each day,
Whether as he moved among twisted oaks,
Or glimpsed the rocky confines of a beach,
Or walked through the halls
Among the brilliant feathers of the students,
Or at his drawing board,

Or at his press,
Led to some impulse for creation,
Down to the careful construction of his sentences.

And he moved tirelessly, without effort,
Between our world and his.
As he did when in the metal confines
Of his tank, reeking with sweat
And gasoline and cordite
And the din and rattle of his monster.
He crept up through the carnage
Of the Italian campaign,
Remembered now through his print
Of a mountain-top monastery
In lines and shades coloured subtly
And rugged with those ancient stones.

Creation was his breath;
He breathed so all his life,
Always fascinated by the idea,
And then the way to bring that view to life
In all its myriad forms—
A painting thick in oils or wet with colour,
A print, the lines and hues boldly attacked,
An etching impressed with his imprint,
His home, rich with the perfume of his own design,
A Japanese restaurant that caught the orient,
The signature of his furniture.
The grace of his sailing boats,
The rich succession of his stage designs and costumes,
The intricacies of all technical things,
Oiled, coiled, geared, and useful,
Or the pixel flicker of the monitor
Prompted by the subterranean flashes
Of its electronic master.

And always he had two compelling voices:
His own patient voice
And his hand with pencil or pen,
Both working in chorus.
The readiness was all
To wrench again something from our world,
His utility belt always around his waist,
Another skin, another limb
Always in use.

He did not need the old gods and figures
To keep him company;
He lived in comfort
With other artists around him,
Or technicians,
Or mechanics—
Any artisan.
And at the centre
Of that thick coil of friends
Were his wife and children,
Supporting him in all his many urges,
Giving him the true home
For starting out on each new quest
And his return.

But with all his glittering facets
It was the entire diamond lustre
Of his teaching that lights us all.
No student, either groping through
An adolescent and a novice thicket
Or as a young adult flexing
An artistic muscle or two,
Was unchanged from working with him.
He led them with patience and example
To their own vision of this world
And what they must do to find
Their own way of expressing it.

So he worked,
And so he reaps
Through family and friend and student
The harvest of his life-long art
Passed on to others
Even as we use his example here
In praise of him.

Music was his breath

Music was his breath
He inhaled atmospheres around him
exhaled landscapes across oceans
bright with African and prairie sun
white with blizzards
dark with rattled gales

Within his countries
he discovered the ululations of winds
snares' thickets
by percussion's reverberating hills
the sonorous blasts of brass
against the deep bass throbbing
throughout his sounding forests
the dark-throated cello's cry
and the rustled sighing of the strings

Rhythm nestled and surged in his blood
crept nervously under the strings' conversations
skittered mischievously through their whisperings
beat against the crowding words of choruses
at home in dark foliage-hidden beats
or with the calculated stresses
of a distant century's cavalier
toying with his golden nymphs

Word and meaning sang to him
and he sang back
lifting their two voices in the sentient air
enveloping both in a vibrant stream of notes
or teasing them with sly arrangement

Sudden discoveries mark his terrain
vistas open miraculously
or wrench without warning
in perilous curves
and abrupt changes
perspectives expand before us
or fade and disappear
logic and surprise teasing each other

Challenges attracted and exhilarated him
to collect for his own world
the humble wheezing of an instrument
animals in childish rhymes
the vastness of a continent
the glory of a daughter's bow

Humour tinged his utterance
shone in his eye and his sharp ear
his passions lay deep
his enthusiasms rich and multifarious
his teaching lucid and inspiring

Complex himself and the routes he carved
yet his maps remain precise and clear
unfolding revelations
to those who explore them
and translate luminously to us
as do his person and his music echo
vivid in our memory

The whispered quiver of the leaf

The whispered quiver of the leaf,
The sighed murmur of the winded forest,
Were the conversations she grew to love,
Felt in the sympathetic tremor of her muscles,
In the rhythmic attachment of her heart.

Nor was there ever true solitude,
For her cats played shadows about the cabin
And among the radiant flowers and cool grasses,
The coated sheep accepted docilely her friendship,
The horses nuzzled her graceful gifted fingers,
Joining her in the dance with the slow wheeling seasons.

So different from the mirrored studios,
The unforgiving barre and the unyielding floor,
Protesting muscles forced to obedience,
And the currents of the dance swept into the blood
In those young and leaping years
So filled with the rhythmic twists
Of new and long dead choreographers.

Then the shift to help others find each body's place
In space and time and ordered impulse,
To let unfettered and innocent young
Find delight in their own extravagance
Of play in all the shapes and gestures,
In all the provocation of music and step,
Stretching themselves and the boundaries of their world.

So went her pavane of years,
The step made intricate by her tripartite needs:
To find the peace of earth and sea and animal,
To lead others on the dancing quest,
And, deeply embedded in her heart and soul,
The urge to perform outside the framework
Of her moving discipline.

At times these forces warred with each other,
The yearning to perform thwarted
By her island acres green isolation,
Her teaching by the travel and the time.
But through all these travails she kept on,
Graceful in form, gentle in aspect,
Sensitive in understanding and in sympathy
To all those around her, animal and human.

And her outward form and manner belied
Her inner strength and toughness.
Once, when her citadel of bones
Was shattered, broken to the point of death,
Her will forced each breath against the broken ribs,
Despite the tortured agony incurred,
Until at last a healing could take place.

Never did she surrender, either before,
Or then, or later; always she worked
To move forward, whether with the land
Or with herself. Yet sometimes her love
Of those around her led her to unexpected places:
Her flock grew old and arthritic, and some
Ancient wooly friends died quietly in her arms.

At times her life was wrenched with harsh disappointment
And betrayal; but of these times she kept silent,
Keeping such anguish to herself, with too much integrity
To complain.

As her dance came to its end, her mind waltzed away,
And then her life.

Now let the waves on the shore below her cabin
Lap quietly her name;
Let the trees sway their devotion,
And the murmurs and the whispers
Of her plants and pastures keep alive
Her name and memory.

She is dead now, in her nineties

She is dead now, in her nineties,
peacefully in her sleep, slipping away
as quietly as memory
glided from her daily, leaving her
with each fresh moment minted new just to
evaporate with the next, in mind and out.
Nothing left at the end but her familiar chuckle
and bright, infectious laugh, still a girl's,
and the reflection of the twinkle in the eye.

What did she leave?
Ancient brothers and sisters to follow her,
dead sisters and brothers whom she follows,
and her husband also,
two children, and their children,
and myriad nieces, nephews, second cousins,
the whole panoply and stew of family and relations.

Now she is memory only,
body back to dust and ashes,
no tomb or marker to identify her living place.

Why then remember her?
Why search among the fragments
and the labyrinth of my memory
to jigsaw her again to life?

In each life someone may insinuate
into our fibres connections
that can never be detached or wrenched
from their familiar, submerged resting place.
She was my aunt, my father's sister,
my mother's brother's wife.
She was always there for me
when I was young or old.

Not like my uncle, with thinning hair,
perpetual bureaucratic lines of care
etched into forehead and mouth's corners,
brooding in armchair, who filled the place
of father when my own was off to war,
with whom I had a wary, loving dependence,
with whom I fought and argued, struggled over math,
helped to roll cigarettes with an ingenious machine,
made survey plans, dug pits on survey crews,
and cherished as my namesake.

Her image now slips just beyond
the verge of memory, in and out of focus.
Only the catalogue of features
keeps her together:
Dark hair, a pleasant handsome Irish face,
lips always curved for smile
or laughter, erect posture,
and innate dignity.

My aunt and I lived together in our laughter.
After school, on weekends, in her kitchen
boy and woman found a merry world,
full of fantastic and bizarre delights
to chuckle at, to share, to invent together,
a patchwork pastiche, pinned and punned,
a world apart from war and trouble,
just ours and ours alone, our own oasis,
no ego here, no competition, just the fun
we made together.

All through our lives we shared this world
although much dimmed with distance
and distraction,
always the world around us could be twisted
by a joke, a twinkle in the eye, a look,
and that other world return, immutable,
still fresh and fragrant with our attitudes.

She will not fade away for me.
An Irish Nora, aptly named—
always in her smile a woman,
always in her love an aunt.

The house is now vacated,
but in my attic mind she still resides,
her image coming suddenly to view,
and, oh, her laugh, her laugh still echoing.

In the dead winter, in the night

In the dead winter, in the night,
Stillness of snow and frozen ground,
Breath labours in the frosty fight,
The hushed season hoards its sound.

Then you were born, then you sparked life,
Shocked from blue to an outraged red,
Lost in aired emptiness and strife
Until new swaddling pacified your dread.

Now, slight, long-limbed, asleep you lie,
First excursion into this new world
At end, and new marvels put by,
Their pennants yet to be unfurled.

Let your tiny universe begin
Its convoluted regency,
Its nested journey sibylline
In your newborn potency.

In the child is found the mother,
In the child is found the father:
From here the portent to another,
From the creation to the author.

May this love that rocks you gently
Sustain your ever changing trail;
May you journey innocently
And this devotion never fail.

Notes

1. The births referred to in the section "Nascence" are those of my grandchildren: Nathan, Lucy, Dylan, Rachel, Emma, and Nicholas.

2. "Lucy's song" was written for my granddaughter. When she was born, her mother asked us to give her a gift which would be opened on her tenth birthday. I wrote the song as a gift to aid her in her growing up.

3. In "Venstøp, Ibsen's childhood home," Old Ibsen remembers his childhood at Venstøp, his father's farm outside Skien in Norway. Ibsen was brought up on this farm, during which time his father became bankrupt.

4. Faster Ploug (a character in the excerpt "Young Ibsen's mad aunt, Faster Ploug, tells him of trolls") was Ibsen's mad aunt who, on this occasion, intercepted the boy Ibsen as he climbed into the attic where he, his brother, and she slept. The *styggemann* (stickman) is a Norwegian monster used to frighten children from going outside on their own. His aunt had mistaken the figure of Death in an etching she found in an old English book kept in a chest in the attic.

5. The events described in the section "A Childish Nature" actually happened to me when I was a child. When I was six, my mother took me on the train from Edmonton to Truro, Nova Scotia. The rest of my childhood was spent in Edmonton and other places in Alberta.

6. The "Nursery Rhymes for Adults" were written after composer Malcolm Forsyth set six of my children's poems to music. At a dinner following a performance of the songs, I suggested to him that we collaborate on some nursery rhymes for adults. I sent him these two, but he had just received a commission for a large piece for the National Arts Centre, which he completed just before his death. Unfortunately, he was never able to turn to these pieces.

7. The poem "At forty, joys of family still exist" was written for my son Kevin.

8. The poem "Now as your years soon reach your summer's end" was written for my son Donovan.

9. The three poems "October lights up for your birthday," "On the steep slope below," and "Still October leaves present their colours" were written for my daughter Moira.

10. "As in the green dappled forest" is a poem to my family.

11. "For all her lives" is a poem to Lanni MacDonald on the occasion of her retirement as a director and actor from the Western Canadian Theatre Company.

12. "His fingers have their own life" is a poem to celebrate the retirement of David Lovett from the University of Alberta's Drama Department. David continues to be a brilliant designer and one of the few designers left who has taught others the technique of continental scene painting, in which the surface is placed on the floor and painted using long brushes. David never had a pen out of his hand; wherever he was, he sketched wonderful characters in the margins of his papers or on any scrap or napkin at hand. The poem is shaped after the logo for the department's Studio Theatre logo, which from a distance looks like a vase, but when seen close is actually two faces silhouetted looking at each other.

13. With the exception of the poem "Henrik Ibsen and his wife Suzannah," the excerpts in the section "The Ibsen Poems," as well as "Music's muse is woman fair (Falk's Song)" found in the "Summer" section, are from my play *The Eagle and the Tiger*, which examines the life of Suzannah and Henrik, whose nicknames for each other were the Eagle and the Tiger, or the Cat and the Bear, respectively.

"Falk's Song" and later excerpts are taken from the soiree scene, in which four characters from his plays are imagined coming to Ibsen's apartment for a social evening: Falk, the young poet from *Love's Comedy*; Selma Sjøblom, a young pianist from *The League of Youth*; Judge Brack from *Hedda Gabler*; and Rebecca West from *Rosmersholm*. Falk improvises his song for Selma.

14. "A paradox, this day of love's exchange" is a valentine written to my wife Clara in our sixty-ninth years.

15. "It is said that lovers fall in love, yes?" is a valentine written in our fiftieth year of marriage.

16. If a valentine could be given any time of the year, then "As the sea that, tireless, buoys the ship" is one given to my wife on her eightieth birthday. Unfortunately, on her actual birthday she did not receive the honour due her, as we were at the Sterling Awards Ceremony in Edmonton, where I was receiving an award on that night. In apology I wrote this poem, which was then published in the *Edmonton Journal*, introduced by the following paragraph.

"But especially I wish to thank my wife Clara, whom I shamefully omitted in my reply. For fifty-seven years she has been my mainstay, support, inspiration, and love. She celebrated her eightieth birthday that night, and as a further late gift I dedicate this sonnet to her."

17. "Sestina for a ninetieth birthday" is a poem in celebration of the ninetieth birthday of Roger Bishop, an extraordinary professor at the early Victoria College and later University of Victoria, who created a fine English Department and initiated the development of the Theatre Department there.

18. "On a hundredth birthday" is a poem in celebration of the hundredth birthday of Alfred Angeltvedt, father of my wife and a farmer well-liked by all in Provost, Alberta. The poem was first published in the *Provost News*.

19. "The flesh and blood are sloughed away" was written in memory of William Duncan West. Bill was the archetypal artisan and artist, and one of the finest teachers I have known. There were few forms of art he had not attempted, especially in print making. He designed and built his own house; he designed a Japanese restaurant; he designed boats; and he was a fine set designer and professor. Always, he had his tool belt on his waist, and students at both the secondary level and at the university loved him dearly.

20. "Music was his breath" was written in memory of Malcolm Forsyth, a major composer, with whom I had the great fortune to work a number of times, both as a performer and as a poet.

21. "The whispered quiver of the leaf" was written in memory of Jacqueline Cecil Sears, a lovely dancer, teacher of movement, and performer. Jacqueline was an original member of the Joffrey Ballet Company, had been a Rockette, and was a superb teacher of movement for every age. She owned a sheep ranch on Gabriola Island, to which she returned after whatever engagement she had. I read the poem at her memorial gathering on a beach near her home, as the water lapped at our feet. A sun dog appeared during the ceremony.

22. "She is dead now, in her nineties" was written in memory of my beloved aunt, who died in a nursing home far from Edmonton, where she had lived for so long, although she had begun life in a homestead not far from Ponoka, Alberta.

About the Author

As well as having had a distinguished career in professional theatre and at various universities, Carl Hare has spent the past twenty years writing. His play *The Eagle and the Tiger* has been successfully produced and is in the archives of the National Library of Norway. His children's poems were set to music by the noted composer Malcolm Forsyth and performed by children's choirs in Edmonton. He received a commission from the National Arts Centre for part of the libretto for Forsyth's *A Ballad of Canada*, performed to acclaim in Ottawa and on tour in London, UK. His poem on Malcolm Forsyth will appear in a forthcoming biography of Forsyth.

www.ingramcontent.com/pod-product-compliance
Lightning Source LLC
LaVergne TN
LVHW052341080426
835508LV00045B/3148